REAL LIFE 101:
The Workbook

Derek Avdul
&
Steve Avdul

G GALT INDUSTRIES LLC

ISBN 0-9747287-1-3

Manufactured in the United States of America

This publication contains the opinions and ideas of the authors and is intended to provide helpful and informative material on the subject matter covered. It is sold with the understanding that the authors and the publisher are not engaged in rendering legal, accounting, or other professional advice. If legal advice or other expert assistance is required, the services of a competent professional should be sought.

The authors and publisher specifically disclaim any responsibility for any liability, loss or risk, personal or otherwise, which is incurred as a consequence, direct or indirectly, of the use and application of any of the contents of this book.

Product or brand names used in this book may be trademarks or registered trademarks. For readability, they may appear in initial capitalization or have been capitalized in the style used by the name claimant. Any use of these names is editorial and does not convey endorsement of or other affiliation with the name claimant. The publisher does not intend to express any judgment as to the validity or legal status of any such proprietary claims.

Cover design by Derek Avdul & Steve Avdul

Published by Galt Industries LLC, Post Office Box 1270, Manhattan Beach, CA 90267
www.galtindustries.com

10 9 8 7 6 5 4

CONTENTS

INTRODUCTION

Real Life 101: The Workbook is the ultimate companion to *Real Life 101: A Guide To Stuff That Actually Matters*. This workbook is meant to be used in conjunction with the book to build on the concepts the book presents in order to make many of life's choices easier keeping in mind your individual situation. It tackles those everyday issues regarding your home, car, health, and finances. Use *Real Life 101: The Workbook* to assist you in making decisions so that you can break down each component and understand everything involved.

Start by reading through the real-world examples that accompany each topic. Whether it's comparing potential apartments to rent, calculating the cost of leasing a car, understanding health insurance, or choosing a credit card, *Real Life 101: The Workbook* spells out the facts in an easy-to-follow manner. As you read through the text, refer to the worksheet or template on the facing page that walks through the components of a given subject on a step-by-step basis. Once you're familiar with the topic based on the example, you'll be ready to apply the information to your own personal situation.

That's when the blank templates and worksheets presented in *Real Life 101: The Workbook* are invaluable. Following the simple, step-by-step instructions allows you to tailor every example to your unique circumstances. The accompanying text steers you through the process of creating individualized worksheets and templates that specifically address those issues facing you. Once completed, you'll have all the facts and figures on one page to simplify your options and provide you with the information you need to make sound, informed decisions.

As you create your own one-of-a-kind, decision-making templates and worksheets, refer to *Real Life 101: A Guide To Stuff That Actually Matters* for greater detail or a fuller, more in-depth description of a given topic. The combination of *Real Life 101: A Guide To Stuff That Actually Matters* and *Real Life 101: The Workbook* will ensure you make educated decisions customized to fit your unique situation.

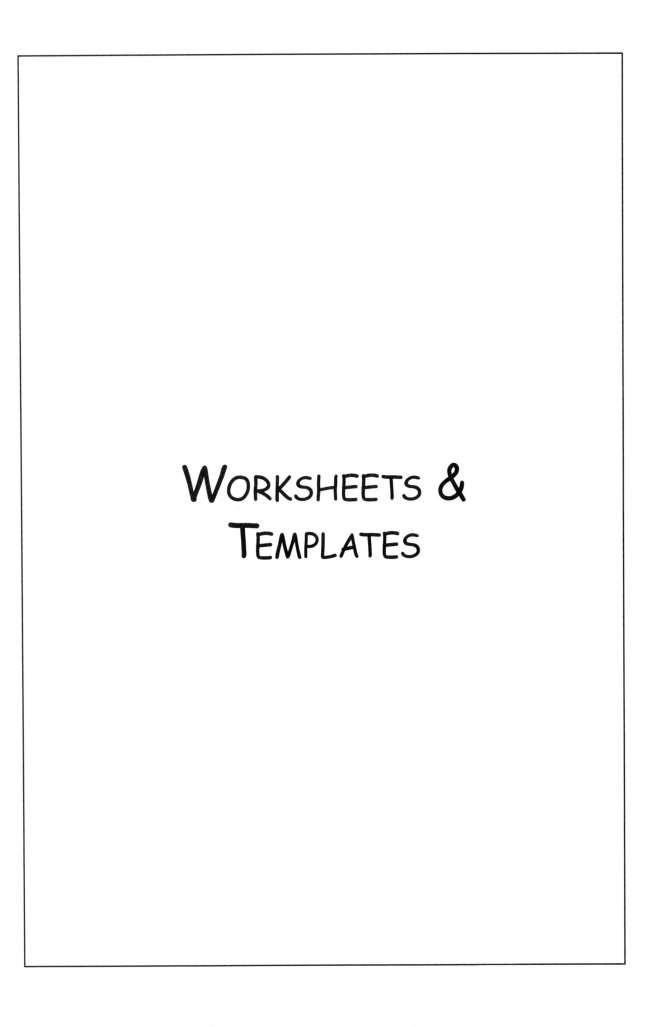

Worksheets & Templates

INITIAL BUDGET WORKSHEET: THE BIG THREE EXPENSES

The three largest monthly expenses for most people are Rent, Car Payment, and Credit Card Payment. This worksheet is designed to allow you to determine what you can realistically afford to spend each month on these items. This is what budgeting is all about. This worksheet presents a range of Recommended Percentages of Gross Income for each of The Big Three Expenses. The example on the facing page walks through both scenarios: the "Low End" and the "High End" of this range.

First, record your Annual Gross Income. Recall that your Gross Income is how much you make before taxes and other items are taken out of your paycheck (i.e., your salary of $24,000 per year or your wage of $12.00 per hour). In the example, Annual Gross Income is $24,000. Divide this by 12 to determine your Monthly Gross Income of $2,000.

Now that you have determined your Monthly Gross Income, apply this $2,000 figure to the Recommended Percentage of Gross Income for each of The Big Three. Start with Rent. In the Low End example, the recommended percentage is 25% so multiply $2,000 x 25% or 0.25 and you get $500. This is how much you should spend each month on your Rent.

Next move to Car Payment. Multiply the $2,000 times the recommended percentage for Car Payment of 10% (in the Low End example) and you get $200 per month for your Car Payment ($2,000 x 10% or 0.10 = $200).

Apply the same procedure to Credit Card Payment. In the Low End example, the recommended percentage for Credit Card Payment is 0% which when multiplied with $2,000 equals $0.

The example then makes the same three calculations for the High End recommended percentages. For Rent it's simply $2,000 x 30% or 0.30 = $600. For Car Payment it's $2,000 x 15% or 0.15 = $300. And for Credit Card Payment it's $2,000 x 5% or 0.05 = $100.

Finally, the example concludes by displaying the recommended range for each of The Big Three. If you earn $24,000 a year or $2,000 a month, you should spend between $500–$600 on your Rent, between $200–$300 on your Car Payment, and between $0–$100 on your Credit Card Payment.

Annual Gross Income: $24,000

Months Per Year ÷ 12

Monthly Gross Income: $2,000

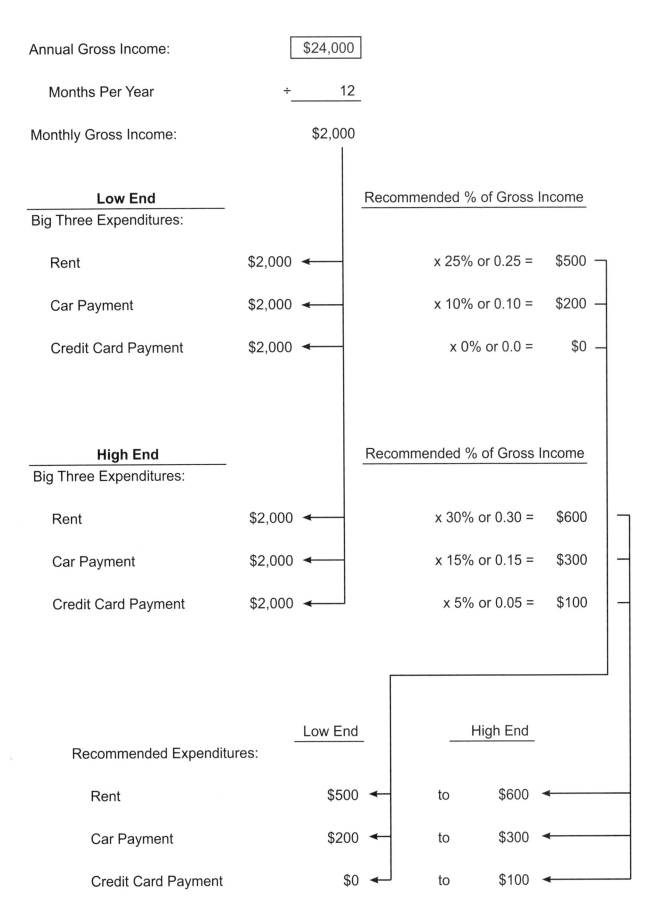

Low End

Big Three Expenditures: Recommended % of Gross Income

Rent $2,000 ← x 25% or 0.25 = $500

Car Payment $2,000 ← x 10% or 0.10 = $200

Credit Card Payment $2,000 ← x 0% or 0.0 = $0

High End

Big Three Expenditures: Recommended % of Gross Income

Rent $2,000 ← x 30% or 0.30 = $600

Car Payment $2,000 ← x 15% or 0.15 = $300

Credit Card Payment $2,000 ← x 5% or 0.05 = $100

Recommended Expenditures:	Low End		High End
Rent	$500	to	$600
Car Payment	$200	to	$300
Credit Card Payment	$0	to	$100

CREATE YOUR OWN WORKSHEET

INITIAL BUDGET WORKSHEET: THE BIG THREE EXPENSES

Start with Annual Gross Income. Put your annual salary in the top box. If you are not paid an annual salary but instead are paid an hourly wage, no problem. Say you make $9.00 per hour. The average American works approximately 2,000 hours each year based on working 40 hours per week for 50 weeks a year (with two weeks off for vacation, holidays, sick days, etc.) So multiply $9.00 per hour times 2,000 hours and you should expect to earn $18,000 each year. If you work overtime on a consistent basis and receive pay for your overtime work, be sure to add this amount to your Annual Gross Income.

Now that you have your Annual Gross Income, divide this number by 12 and put the result on the line next to Monthly Gross Income. Follow the arrow and write this same Monthly Gross Income on the next six blank lines beside Rent, Car Payment, and Credit Card Payment in both the Low End and High End examples.

Start with the first of the six Monthly Gross Income numbers and apply the recommended percentage. For Rent in the Low End example, multiply your Monthly Gross Income times 25% or 0.25 and write the result on the blank line to the right. Next is Car Payment, so multiply the same Monthly Gross Income figure times 10% or 0.10 and write that result on the blank line to the right as well. Continue down the page with Credit Card Payment and then repeat all three calculations using the new percentages in the High End example.

Finally take the six results from the lines on the right-hand side of the page and follow the arrows down to the bottom and place each of the six results on its corresponding line at the bottom of the page. Now you have a completed worksheet and have a range of recommended amounts to spend per month for each of The Big Three items.

Annual Gross Income: ☐

Months Per Year ÷ _____ 12

Monthly Gross Income: _____

Low End

Big Three Expenditures: | Recommended % of Gross Income

Rent _____ ← | x 25% or 0.25 = _____

Car Payment _____ ← | x 10% or 0.10 = _____

Credit Card Payment _____ ← | x 0% or 0.0 = _____

High End

Big Three Expenditures: | Recommended % of Gross Income

Rent _____ ← | x 30% or 0.30 = _____

Car Payment _____ ← | x 15% or 0.15 = _____

Credit Card Payment _____ ← | x 5% or 0.05 = _____

	Low End	High End
Recommended Expenditures:		
Rent	_____	to _____
Car Payment	_____	to _____
Credit Card Payment	_____	to _____

MONTHLY EXPENSE WORKSHEET

Many people run up a lot of debt or get into financial trouble because they don't have a handle on their expenses. They know what their rent and car cost each month, and they certainly pay their utilities and phone bill, but really don't know exactly how much money they are actually spending. This worksheet is designed to allow you to understand where your money is going. It will help you determine if you are living within your means or are spending too much and could be headed for financial trouble in the future.

Start with Household Expenses. In this example Rent, Utilities, and Food total $694. Car Expenses include not only the Car Payment of $225 but also Car Insurance, Car Maintenance, and Gas which brings the total to $325. A Store Credit Card and a regular Credit Card bring this category to $90. Each of these subtotals is then entered at the bottom of the worksheet next to its corresponding category heading and arrow.

On the right side of the page, Healthcare Expenses are summed and the total of $75 is also entered at the bottom of the page. Note the category of Other Expenses includes whatever other regular expenses you have such as a Cell Phone, Clothes, Dining, and Entertainment. If you have regular or predictable expenses in these categories, list them here. The total of $220 is then entered at the bottom.

The last category on the sheet is Taxes. In this example, the amount is $500 or 25% of the Monthly Gross Income of $2,000. If you don't know exactly how much you pay in taxes each month, a good rule of thumb is 25% of your Monthly Gross Income.

Finally, once all the categories have been totaled and the results transferred to the bottom of the page, simply subtract each subtotal from Monthly Gross Income. In this case, subtracting $694, $325, $90, $75, $220, and $500 from $2,000 leaves the person with $96 each month for savings or free spending.

Remember, however, that this example built in $45 each month for Dining, $50 for Clothes, and another $90 for Entertainment and Miscellaneous in the Other Expenses category. If all of these amounts were $0, the person would have $281 each month to do whatever he or she wanted which could include some of these same entertainment activities.

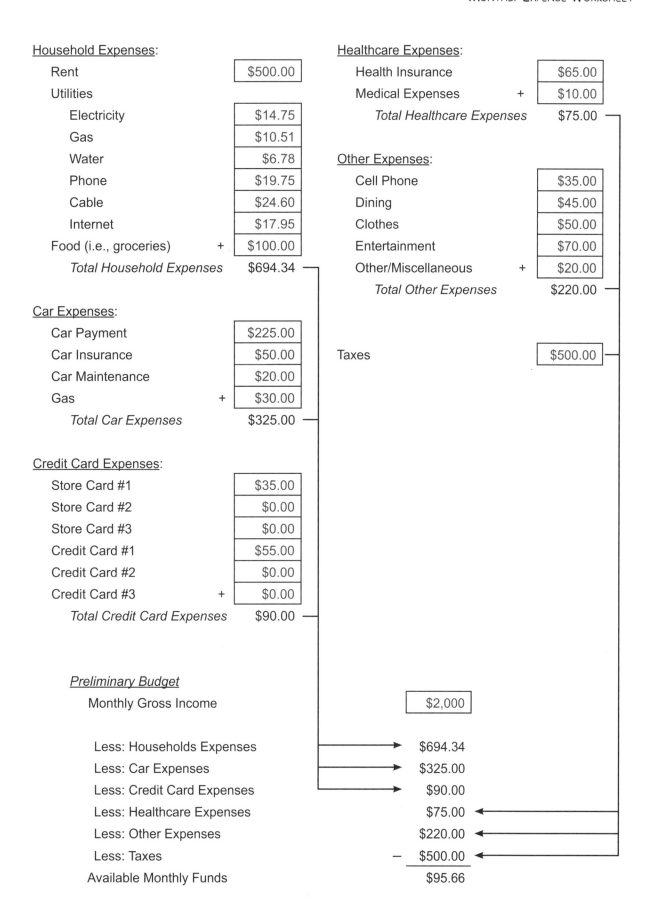

Household Expenses:

Rent	$500.00
Utilities	
Electricity	$14.75
Gas	$10.51
Water	$6.78
Phone	$19.75
Cable	$24.60
Internet	$17.95
Food (i.e., groceries) +	$100.00
Total Household Expenses	$694.34

Car Expenses:

Car Payment	$225.00
Car Insurance	$50.00
Car Maintenance	$20.00
Gas +	$30.00
Total Car Expenses	$325.00

Credit Card Expenses:

Store Card #1	$35.00
Store Card #2	$0.00
Store Card #3	$0.00
Credit Card #1	$55.00
Credit Card #2	$0.00
Credit Card #3 +	$0.00
Total Credit Card Expenses	$90.00

Healthcare Expenses:

Health Insurance	$65.00
Medical Expenses +	$10.00
Total Healthcare Expenses	$75.00

Other Expenses:

Cell Phone	$35.00
Dining	$45.00
Clothes	$50.00
Entertainment	$70.00
Other/Miscellaneous +	$20.00
Total Other Expenses	$220.00

Taxes	$500.00

Preliminary Budget

Monthly Gross Income	$2,000
Less: Households Expenses	$694.34
Less: Car Expenses	$325.00
Less: Credit Card Expenses	$90.00
Less: Healthcare Expenses	$75.00
Less: Other Expenses	$220.00
Less: Taxes	− $500.00
Available Monthly Funds	$95.66

CREATE YOUR OWN WORKSHEET

MONTHLY EXPENSE WORKSHEET

Grab all your regular monthly bills, a pencil, and a calculator—time to figure your monthly spending. Some expenses can be a little tricky since they can vary from month to month. The phone bill, for example, can move up or down depending on the amount of long distance calls. Add up the past three months of phone bills and divide the total by three and you'll have the average amount per month. Do this for each Household Expense as necessary and fill in the remaining line items. Record the sum of all the lines next to Total Household Expenses. Be sure to follow the arrow down and enter this same amount again.

Car Expenses are relatively straightforward with the possible exception of gas. You may need to estimate based on how much it costs to fill up your tank and how many times a month you fill it up. For example, if it costs you $20 to fill the tank and you usually do it every other week, you're spending about $40 a month on gas. Total the Car Expenses and again repeat the result at the bottom of the page. Continue this exercise for Credit Card Expenses, Healthcare Expenses, and Other Expenses.

Entertainment or Dining expenses may be tough to figure. Some people have a good feel for the amount they spend on these types of items and feel comfortable entering an amount on these line items. Other people would prefer not to think of these expenses as "monthly" expenses and instead use whatever money is leftover after paying all their bills as the entertainment "budget" for that month. If you are this latter type of person, put $0 in all these types of line items.

For your Taxes, take a look at your paycheck. If you have a monthly pay stub, the amount you pay in taxes is readily apparent—just be sure to include all the taxes. If you receive a weekly paycheck, simply multiply the amount you pay each week by four and you will have a reasonable estimate of how much tax you pay on a monthly basis. Another good way to estimate your monthly tax expense is to take your Monthly Gross Income and multiply it by 25% (or 0.25).

Once everything is filled in, move to the bottom of the worksheet to finish the calculation. Take your Monthly Gross Income and subtract all the expense subtotals and see what your Available Monthly Funds are. If you already included entertainment expenses in the Other Expenses category, this is the amount you have left for savings or whatever else you want to do with it. If you entered $0 in the Other Expenses categories, now you know exactly how much you can spend on Entertainment, Dining, Clothes, etc.

Household Expenses:

Rent ☐

Utilities

    Electricity ☐

    Gas ☐

    Water ☐

    Phone ☐

    Cable ☐

    Internet ☐

Food (i.e., groceries)   + ☐

Total Household Expenses _____

Car Expenses:

    Car Payment ☐

    Car Insurance ☐

    Car Maintenance ☐

    Gas   + ☐

Total Car Expenses _____

Credit Card Expenses:

    Store Card #1 ☐

    Store Card #2 ☐

    Store Card #3 ☐

    Credit Card #1 ☐

    Credit Card #2 ☐

    Credit Card #3   + ☐

Total Credit Card Expenses _____

Healthcare Expenses:

    Health Insurance ☐

    Medical Expenses   + ☐

Total Healthcare Expenses _____

Other Expenses:

    Cell Phone ☐

    Dining ☐

    Clothes ☐

    Entertainment ☐

    Other/Miscellaneous   + ☐

Total Other Expenses _____

Taxes ☐

Preliminary Budget

    Monthly Gross Income ☐

    Less: Households Expenses _____

    Less: Car Expenses _____

    Less: Credit Card Expenses _____

    Less: Healthcare Expenses _____

    Less: Other Expenses _____

    Less: Taxes   − _____

  Available Monthly Funds _____

APARTMENT COMPARISON TEMPLATE

When looking for apartments it can be difficult to remember exactly which apartment had what features and all the plusses and minuses of an individual unit. While you're physically inside each apartment you may think you'll remember everything but after a day traipsing through half a dozen places, recalling the specifics of each apartment can be confusing. You need an Apartment Comparison Template.

Start with the General Apartment Information. You can usually get this information before you've even seen the place. Most of the data is almost always included in the ad in the paper, on the web site, or can be given to you over the phone. Make sure you fill in this information before going to see the apartment itself. There is really no point in wasting your time looking at a three-bedroom apartment that costs $1,200 if you only need a one-bedroom or can only afford $500 a month. Be sure to consider the amount of Money Due at Move-In when making your decision among apartments. This amount will include first month's rent, a security deposit and/or pet deposit, and miscellaneous fees. Use the Money Due At Move-In Worksheet on page 31 to compute this amount.

The Apartment Features section includes any and all of the amenities that may be important to you when selecting an apartment. Some will obviously mean more to you than others. Note that some of the features are simply "yes" or "no" as to whether the apartment has them such as Central Air Conditioning or a Dishwasher. Other amenities require you to judge for yourself as to the quality such as the amount of Natural Light in Unit or Closet Space. Try to be consistent with your assessment as you move from apartment to apartment so you'll have an "apples-to-apples" comparison at the end of the day.

Continue this ranking and recording of the apartment's features for both the Community/Building as well as the surrounding Neighborhood. If you're torn between two apartments with nearly identical features within the apartment, often times the amenities of the apartment complex such as a swimming pool or the location of the building near your work or close to great restaurants can be enough to break the tie. Be sure to evaluate the apartment on these aspects as well.

	Apartment #1
General Apartment Information:	
Address	123 Main St
Number of Bedrooms	1
Number of Bathrooms	1.5
Square Footage	925
Utilities Included	Gas
Monthly Rent	$500
Money Due at Move-in	$800
Apartment Features:	
Location (Basement, Top Floor, etc.)	Top
Central Air Conditioning	Yes
Bedroom Size	Small
Closet Space	Good
Flooring (Carpeting vs. Hardwood)	Carpet
Separate Dining Room/Area	No
Balcony/Deck	Yes
Natural Light in Unit	Good
Fireplace	No
Washer/Dryer Location	No
Refrigerator	Yes
Dishwasher	Yes
Built-in Microwave	Yes
Garbage Disposal	Yes
Community/Building Features:	
Pets Allowed	Yes
Parking	Street
Laundry Facilities	Down hall
Pool/Recreation Facilities	Pool
Neighborhood Features:	
Safety	Good
Proximity to Work/School	Close
Proximity to Shopping	Okay
Proximity to Recreation/Entertainment	Close
Notes	Great Apt. Manager

CREATE YOUR OWN TEMPLATE

APARTMENT COMPARISON TEMPLATE

The value of the Apartment Comparison Template is its ability to compare the characteristics of multiple apartments at the same time. That's why this template has space to list three separate apartments on the same page.

Always start by filling in the General Apartment Information. You can quickly eliminate several apartments that are out of your price range or are not the right size before you even visit them. Plus, there is no point in filling out the rest of the information on the Apartment Comparison Template if the apartment doesn't fit your general criteria for Number of Bedrooms or Monthly Rent.

Have this template with you as you view each apartment and fill in a response to each line item on the spot. It's a great idea to be an "active" rather than "passive" apartment viewer. Being "active" means having this workbook and a pen with you, taking notes, and jotting down your impressions. Do it while you are standing there and things are fresh in your mind rather than trying to remember everything at the end of the day. Don't forget to have a tape measure handy if a copy of the floor plan with room dimensions isn't available.

Some of the line items are straightforward. Simple "Yes" or "No" works for many of the appliance line items. Others require your judgment. Bedroom Size could be "150 sq. ft.," "Medium," or "Okay" depending on how you prefer to do things. There is no right or wrong answer so long as you are consistent for all the apartments you view and compare.

Not every line item on this list will be important to you. If you never plan on building a fire, then the presence of a Fireplace may not warrant bothering to record the information. However, you never know what could turn out to be a deciding factor. You may not have any pets so you might think that Pets Allowed is a category that doesn't matter. But what if everything is tied between two apartments and you can't decide but you noted that one building had several neighbors with loud, barking dogs? You may opt to take the other place in order to ensure a good night's sleep. Factors that may seem unimportant at first can weigh into your decision.

Finally, jot down any notes at the bottom that capture impressions that weren't specifically mentioned elsewhere in the template. This could range from your take on the apartment manager, any "gut feel" about the place, or any interaction or conversation with a neighbor. Remember, the more information you can gather, the better.

	Apartment #1	Apartment #2	Apartment #3
General Apartment Information:			
Address			
Number of Bedrooms			
Number of Bathrooms			
Square Footage			
Utilities Included			
Monthly Rent			
Money Due at Move-in			
Apartment Features:			
Location (Basement, Top Floor, etc.)			
Central Air Conditioning			
Bedroom Size			
Closet Space			
Flooring (Carpeting vs. Hardwood)			
Separate Dining Room/Area			
Balcony/Deck			
Natural Light in Unit			
Fireplace			
Washer/Dryer Location			
Refrigerator			
Dishwasher			
Built-in Microwave			
Garbage Disposal			
Community/Building Features:			
Pets Allowed			
Parking			
Laundry Facilities			
Pool/Recreation Facilities			
Neighborhood Features:			
Safety			
Proximity to Work/School			
Proximity to Shopping			
Proximity to Recreation/Entertainment			
Notes			

RENTAL APPLICATION MATERIALS TEMPLATE

Once you've decided on a place to live, you need to fill out a rental application and provide the landlord with some paperwork about yourself, your job, your finances, and your rental history. It's nothing particularly complicated or involved but it's worth reviewing what information you'll be asked to provide to ensure there are no surprises and that you have all the relevant paperwork.

This template walks through the basic information. The first thing landlords and apartment management companies want to know about you is your current employment. Depending on the situation, you could be asked about both current and previous employers especially if you've only been with a current employer for a short period of time. A good rule of thumb is to have employment information for the prior three years. You should have the basic contact information regarding name and address of the company as well the contact name of a supervisor or boss and that person's phone number. The example lists this information for both the current job at ABC Corporation as well as for a previous job at XYZ Corporation. You may not be asked to present all of this data but better to be prepared and have it available than to scramble to pull it together at the last minute. Salary information is also requested as landlords want to verify your income to ensure you can afford the apartment.

As with employer information, you'll be asked to provide the name, address, and contact person and phone for current and previous residences. Apartment management companies will almost always verify this information and often check with previous landlords to ensure that you paid your rent on time, were a good tenant, and weren't destructive to the apartment. Make certain you have this information because new landlords are immediately skeptical of prospective renters who fail to provide previous addresses and contacts.

Finally, depending where you live and what type of building you're trying to rent, some rental companies and landlords will require financial information beyond basic salary verification. The example lists pieces of information ranging from social security number to checking and savings account numbers to credit card accounts and balances. You may not need to provide any of this data or you may be asked to list some or even all of the information. This template is designed to prepare you for anything that may be thrown your way. Better to gather it all in a folder and have it with you and never use it than to be sitting in the manager's office about to rent a place only to be denied because you haven't provided enough information.

Employment Information (for last 3 years):

Employer Name	ABC Corporation
Address	123 Fake Street
Address	Suite 0
City, State, Zip Code	LA, CA 99999
Length of Employment	2 years, 4 months
Salary	$24,000
Supervisor	Mrs. Smith
Phone Number	555-5555

Employer Name	XYZ Corporation
Address	456 Fake Street
Address	Suite 0
City, State, Zip Code	LA, CA 99999
Length of Employment	1 year, 3 months
Salary	$22,000
Supervisor	Mr. Jones
Phone Number	555-5555

Previous Residence Information (for last 3 years):

Address	123 Random Street
Address	Apartment 0
City, State, Zip Code	LA, CA 99999
Length at Residence	1 year
Monthly Rent	$450
Landlord	Gotham Management
Phone Number	555-5555

Address	456 Random Street
Address	Unit 0
City, State, Zip Code	LA, CA 99999
Length at Residence	2 years
Monthly Rent	$430
Landlord	City Management
Phone Number	555-5555

Financial Information:

Social Security Number	123-45-6789
Checking Account Bank	Bank of America
Checking Account Number	12345-67890
Savings Account Bank	None
Savings Account Number	--
Credit Card #1 Name	MBNA Visa
Credit Card #1 Number	2222-2222-2222-2222
Credit Card #1 Balance	$100
Credit Card #2 Name	Capital One Visa
Credit Card #2 Number	5555-5555-5555-5555
Credit Card #2 Balance	$250

CREATE YOUR OWN TEMPLATE

RENTAL APPLICATION MATERIALS TEMPLATE

The easiest way to ensure that you have everything you need when applying to rent an apartment is to fill out this template in advance. Start by gathering the necessary information to prepare your own Rental Application Materials Template.

The Employment Information is usually easy enough to pull together and one of the simplest ways is to grab your latest pay stub. It will almost certainly list your employer's address and phone. Plus it provides verification of your salary. You'll need to provide the missing details of your Supervisor's name as well as the Length of Employment at your current job.

It can be slightly trickier to track down this information for a previous employer. Again, a copy of an old pay stub works best but if that is not available, there are other ways. Your W–2 (the income tax form you use to complete your taxes) will contain most of the relevant data. You can always look up your former employer in the phone book or online. If you can't remember your supervisor's name or if that person no longer works there, don't worry about it, just try to provide as much information as possible.

Previous Residence Information can be more difficult than first anticipated. If you've moved a couple of times in recent years, or have shared apartments with friends, there can appear to be information gaps. A three-year residence history is usually enough but sometimes landlords will go back as far as five years. Again, filling out this template in advance will quickly alert you to your own lack of complete information. Maybe you've forgotten an old zip code. Better to take ten minutes now and look it up online or to find an old piece of mail with your address on it than to be sitting in the manager's office trying to pull the number out of the air. Even if you shared an apartment with others and your name was not on the apartment lease, you should still have the relevant information.

While every application will definitely ask for employment and residence information, the requirement for certain financial information is less certain. Go ahead and get a bank statement as well as credit card statement and jot down the relevant data on this template. You may not need to provide this information but it doesn't hurt to have it with you.

The point is to pull all of the above information in advance and use it to fill in this template. Place all of the paperwork and this completed template in a manila folder and you're all set. Take that folder with you when you go to look for an apartment and you'll be certain to be able to complete any apartment rental application without a hitch.

Employment Information (for last 3 years):

Employer Name _____

Address _____

Address _____

City, State, Zip Code _____

Length of Employment _____

Salary _____

Supervisor _____

Phone Number _____

Employer Name _____

Address _____

Address _____

City, State, Zip Code _____

Length of Employment _____

Salary _____

Supervisor _____

Phone Number _____

Previous Residence Information (for last 3 years):

Address _____

Address _____

City, State, Zip Code _____

Length at Residence _____

Monthly Rent _____

Landlord _____

Phone Number _____

Address _____

Address _____

City, State, Zip Code _____

Length at Residence _____

Monthly Rent _____

Landlord _____

Phone Number _____

Financial Information:

Social Security Number _____

Checking Account Bank _____

Checking Account Number _____

Savings Account Bank _____

Savings Account Number _____

Credit Card #1 Name _____

Credit Card #1 Number _____

Credit Card #1 Balance _____

Credit Card #2 Name _____

Credit Card #2 Number _____

Credit Card #2 Balance _____

QUALIFYING FOR AN APARTMENT WORKSHEET

How do landlords and apartment management companies decide who gets an apartment and who is turned down? There is actually some method to their madness. By completing this worksheet, you'll be able to determine, in advance, whether you're likely to be approved for certain apartments.

Landlords usually work backwards when determining which prospective tenants make good candidates. They start with the Monthly Rent on the apartment of $500. Multiply this by 12 and you have the Total Annual Rent of $6,000. This is simple enough.

Now is when apartment rental companies exercise a little discretion. They use a figure entitled Annual Rent as a % of Gross Income. In other words, they determine a level of income necessary to afford a given apartment. When creating the Initial Budget Worksheet, it was presented that spending between 25%–30% of your Gross Income on Rent was an appropriate range. These figures were not made up out of thin air. They were chosen largely because this is traditionally what landlords have deemed an acceptable level. Landlords worry that if half your money (i.e., 50%) were earmarked for Rent, you'd have too many other expenses competing for your paycheck so you wouldn't actually be able to pay Rent. Keep in mind the higher the percentage landlords allow, the lower the amount of income you'll need to be able to afford the apartment.

In the example, the Total Annual Rent was $6,000. The next line item is Annual Rent as a % of Gross Income and the corresponding figure is 30%. Note that the column heading is entitled "Higher Percentage of Income" since 30% is at the high end of the 25%–30% range. Take the $6,000 and divide it by 30% and the result is $20,000. That is, you need an Income Necessary to Afford This Apartment of $20,000. As a check, multiply $20,000 times 30% and you get $6,000 or exactly the amount of Annual Rent.

The above calculations are repeated in the second half of the example. This time the lower Annual Rent as a % of Gross Income of 25% is used. Note that dividing $6,000 by 25% equals $24,000. This means that if the landlord required that no more than 25% of Gross Income were to be allocated for Rent, then you'd need to earn at least $24,000 to rent the same $500-a-month apartment. Thus, the lower the maximum percentage, the higher the necessary income and vice versa.

Therefore, in this example, you would need to earn between $20,000 and $24,000 to rent this apartment.

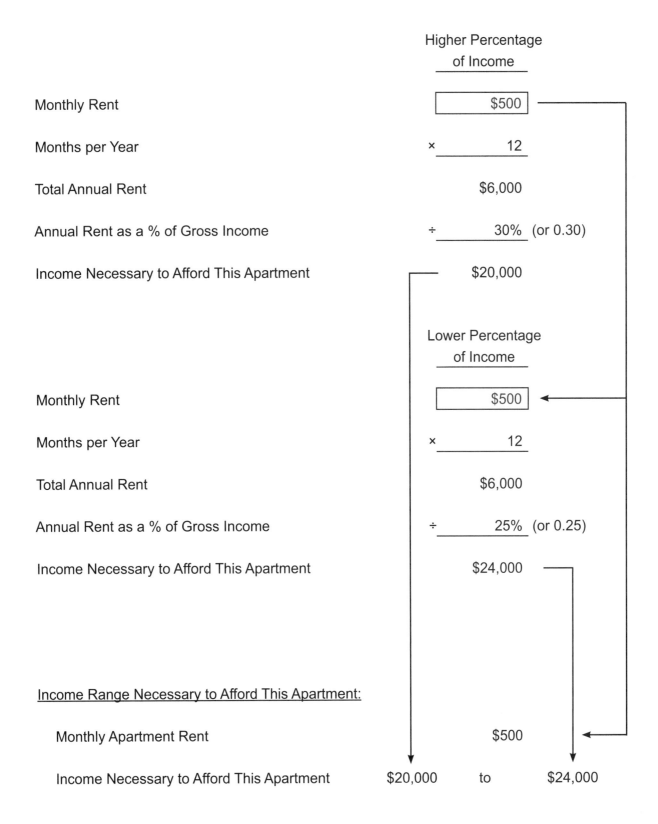

Higher Percentage
of Income

Monthly Rent	$500
Months per Year	× 12
Total Annual Rent	$6,000
Annual Rent as a % of Gross Income	÷ 30% (or 0.30)
Income Necessary to Afford This Apartment	$20,000

Lower Percentage
of Income

Monthly Rent	$500
Months per Year	× 12
Total Annual Rent	$6,000
Annual Rent as a % of Gross Income	÷ 25% (or 0.25)
Income Necessary to Afford This Apartment	$24,000

Income Range Necessary to Afford This Apartment:

Monthly Apartment Rent		$500	
Income Necessary to Afford This Apartment	$20,000	to	$24,000

CREATE YOUR OWN WORKSHEET

QUALIFYING FOR AN APARTMENT WORKSHEET

To see if you qualify for the apartment you want, start by placing the Monthly Rent amount on the first line. Multiply this figure by 12 and you have the Total Annual Rent which is entered in the next blank line. Divide this Total Annual Rent figure by the higher percentage of Gross Income the management company requires (or 30% or 0.30 if none is specified) and you'll have the Income Necessary to Afford This Apartment. Fill that number in on this line item, follow the arrow to the bottom of the page, and reenter the same number in the blank on the left side.

Repeat the same calculations as above in the second set of blanks, substituting only the Annual Rent as a % of Gross Income. That is, divide the Total Annual Rent by the lower percentage of Gross Income the management company requires (or 25% or 0.25 if none is specified). Enter the result on the blank line and again at the bottom of the page on the right side. You now know the range of income the landlord is likely to require to rent the apartment you're considering.

Higher Percentage
of Income
_____

Monthly Rent   [   ]

Months per Year   ×   12

Total Annual Rent   _____

Annual Rent as a % of Gross Income   ÷   30% (or 0.30)

Income Necessary to Afford This Apartment   _____

Lower Percentage
of Income
_____

Monthly Rent   [   ]

Months per Year   ×   12

Total Annual Rent   _____

Annual Rent as a % of Gross Income   ÷   25% (or 0.25)

Income Necessary to Afford This Apartment   _____

Income Range Necessary to Afford This Apartment:

Monthly Apartment Rent   _____

Income Necessary to Afford This Apartment   _____ to _____

MONEY DUE AT MOVE-IN WORKSHEET

Once you've selected an apartment and been approved by the management company, you need to figure out exactly how much money you'll need to move in. Unfortunately, it's not as simple as just showing up on the first of the month with a check for the rent—there are other fees and additional monies that may be required.

Before the landlord will hand you the keys to your new apartment, he or she will require money to cover a variety of issues. The first is Security Deposit, in this example $200, and it serves as the landlord's guarantee that you won't trash the place or damage the apartment during the time you live there. If you do ruin the carpet or break things, the landlord with keep the Security Deposit when you move out and use it to repair the apartment.

The same principle exists for the next item, Pet Deposit. It's an additional amount of security for the landlord given that pets tend to cause more damage than might normally occur without a pet.

Next are First Month's Rent and Last Month's Rent. First Month's Rent is rather self-explanatory—you need to pay the $500 rent before you move in. Nothing shocking here. You may be a little surprised about Last Month's Rent. Some rental properties, not all, require you to prepay a second month's rent in advance, in this case another $500. They do this in case you were to break your lease and move out early. If you do stay for your entire lease, then when the last month of your lease comes, you pay no rent for that month.

Add up all of the above items and you quickly realize that in order to get the keys to your new place, you need to write a check for $1,300. And this is just the amount that you have to give to the landlord. There are still other fees and deposits you may need to pay before moving in.

The next four items are all utility-related expenses and may or may not be required at the time you move in. In the example, you need to give the Cable Company $50 and the Power Company $25. You are able to have the phone and other utilities such as water or gas hooked up without providing a deposit. Typically, Utility Deposits are required for first-time renters—once you've had a utility in your name in that service area, you usually don't need a deposit if you move from one apartment to another.

Finally, when it is all said and done, you need $1,300 to give the landlord and another $75 for the utility companies for a total of $1,375.

Apartment Move-In Fees:

Security Deposit	$200
Pet Deposit*	$100
First Month's Rent	$500
Last Month's Rent*	+ $500
Total For Apartment	$1,300

Utility Company Fees:

Cable Company*	$50
Power Company*	$25
Phone Company*	$0
Other Utilities*	+ $0
Total For Utilities	$75

Money Due At Move-In:

Total For Apartment	$1,300
Total For Utilities	+ $75
Money Due At Move-In	$1,375

may or may not be required

CREATE YOUR OWN WORKSHEET

MONEY DUE AT MOVE-IN WORKSHEET

Before moving into a new apartment, you need to figure out how much cash you have to plunk down just to get the keys from the landlord. Not only is this important so that you are sure you can actually afford the place but also because the Money Due At Move-In can be a source of differentiation when choosing apartments. Recall that the Apartment Comparison Template has a line item entitled "Money Due at Move-In." This worksheet is designed to enable you to calculate that amount.

Start with the required Security Deposit. When calling landlords regarding potential apartments, ask for this amount. Enter that on the first line. Also, if you have a pet, you may be required to post a Pet Deposit as well. If applicable, enter that amount on the second line; otherwise, enter $0.

Every rental company will require your First Month's Rent before you get the keys so this is an easy one to enter. Last Month's Rent may or may not be required, so like the Security Deposit and Pet Deposit, ask if Last Month's Rent is required up front. If it is, enter the same monthly rent amount on this line; otherwise, enter $0.

Add up the four apartment items and place the total on the Total For Apartment line as well as following the arrow down to the bottom and entering the same figure again.

Whether you're moving to a new city or just across town, inquire with the landlord or property manager as to which utility companies provide service to your new apartment building. Even if you've lived in a town for quite a while and are making a short move, you may be surprised to learn that you could be using a different utility provider in the new place. The landlord should provide you with a list of all the utility companies. When you call all of them to schedule the start of service or appointments for installation, ask about any deposits that may be required. This is particularly true for Cable and perhaps Power. Other Utilities such as a cable modem or DSL may also require deposits for equipment. As you speak with each company, enter any deposit amounts required next to the corresponding line item. Add up all the items to get the Total For Utilities and enter it both as a subtotal as well as further down the page by following the arrow.

Finally, add the Total For Apartment and the Total For Utilities and you'll know exactly how much the Money Due At Move-In is so that you can be sure you have enough money to cover everything.

Apartment Move-In Fees:

Security Deposit

Pet Deposit*

First Month's Rent

Last Month's Rent*   +

    Total For Apartment

Utility Company Fees:

Cable Company*

Power Company*

Phone Company*

Other Utilities*   +

    Total For Utilities

Money Due At Move-In:

Total For Apartment

Total For Utilities   +

    Money Due At Move-In

may or may not be required

MASTER PACKING LIST TEMPLATE

Moving can be an incredibly hectic time so the only way to come through the process and still maintain your sanity is to be as organized as possible. The best way to do this is by creating a Master Packing List—it's the key to ensuring you pack everything as efficiently as possible and that everything you own makes it from Point A to Point B without getting lost or misplaced en route.

The concept is simple enough, it's the execution that's the hard part. Too many people don't bother making a list on the front end of the move or checking off every item on the back end and end up losing valuable items during their move. This template will ensure that doesn't happen to you.

As you can see in the example, the list is organized by room and lists both individual pieces of furniture as well as smaller items that will no doubt be boxed up. A simple check mark in the "Packed" column next to Couch, TV, Living Room Box 2, etc. lets you know you haven't forgotten anything.

Some rooms like the kitchen will have fewer furniture items but will have several boxes. Note that it is a good idea to be specific about the contents of each box such as "Kitchen Box 1: Pots and Pans." This detail will come in handy when you actually load each box into the moving van. Bad idea to put your TV on top of the Plates and Glasses box.

The example works through each and every room in your apartment and covers all items ranging from your bed to all your clothes to bathroom toiletries to miscellaneous sports equipment. Be detailed. Cover everything. Go ahead and jot it all down on the Master Packing List—it's the only way valuables are not left behind or lost in the shuffle.

With this level of organization, unpacking becomes a snap. Clearly-labeled boxes and a detailed Master Packing List allow you to easily place each piece of furniture or cardboard box in its proper room. A quick checkmark next to each item and you can rest assured that nothing of value is sitting back at your old place or was left in the parking lot.

	Packed	Delivered
Living Room:		
Couch	√	√
Chairs	√	√
End Table	√	√
TV	√	√
Stereo	√	√
DVD/VCR	√	√
Lamps	√	√
Living Room Box 1: DVDs/CDs	√	√
Living Room Box 2: Books/Misc.	√	√
Kitchen/Dining Room:		
Table	√	√
Chairs	√	√
Microwave	√	√
Coffee Maker	√	√
Kitchen Box 1: Pots and Pans	√	√
Kitchen Box 2: Plates and Glasses	√	√
Kitchen Box 3: Cleaning Supplies	√	√
Bedroom:		
Mattress and Box Spring	√	√
Bed Frame/Headboard	√	√
Dresser	√	√
Bedside Table	√	√
Lamps	√	√
Bedroom Box 1: Wardrobe Box	√	√
Bedroom Box 2: Clothes	√	√
Bedroom Box 3: Clothes	√	√
Bedroom Box 4: Clothes	√	√
Bathroom:		
Bathroom Box 1: Towels and Toiletries	√	√
Bathroom Box 2: Miscellaneous	√	√
Miscellaneous:		
Computer	√	√
File Cabinet	√	√
Sports Equipment	√	√

CREATE YOUR OWN TEMPLATE

MASTER PACKING LIST TEMPLATE

Start making your Master Packing List before you even begin to pack. First list the larger items and pieces of furniture on a room-by-room basis. It's quick and easy to jot down your couch, chairs, tables, and TV in the living room; the table, chairs, and microwave in the kitchen; and the bed, dresser, and bedside table in the bedroom. Add any miscellaneous items such as a computer, desk, or sports equipment and you'll have a complete list of those items you'll be moving but won't be boxing up.

Once you've listed all the larger items, it's on to step two. You actually have to start physically placing smaller, loose items into cardboard boxes. Go room by room and keep things separated. It doesn't make sense to pack pillowcases in the same box with a frying pan, your stereo, and bath towels. As you finish a box, say your CD collection, clearly label it on the front, upper-left corner of the box. Then list this box on the Master Packing List as "Living Room Box 1: CDs." Continue boxing up items, labeling them, and listing each box on the Master Packing List.

As you go room by room, you'll be working down the Master Packing List, filling out the contents of each room by recording the boxed items underneath the furniture items already on the list. By the time everything is boxed up, you'll have a complete Master Packing List and you'll be able to check off each item as you load it into the truck.

As you pull away from your old place, you'll be confident that every item of value you have has been properly catalogued and is making the journey with you to your new place. Once there, it's easy to check off each item as "Delivered" as you place each piece of furniture and box in its proper room. By being organized and paying attention to the small details, you've ensured that your move is as hassle-free as possible and every worldly good you own found its way to your new apartment.

	Packed	Delivered

Living Room:

_____

Kitchen/Dining Room:

_____

Bedroom:

_____

Bathroom:

_____

Miscellaneous:

_____

PROFESSIONAL MOVERS WORKSHEET

So you've decided to go the way of hiring professional movers. Good for you! Better yet, good for your back! Before you start celebrating your good fortune, there are several things to cover to ensure that your wallet doesn't take the pain you're saving your back.

Start by getting answers to general questions regarding Pricing Methodology, Number of Movers, Type of Payment Required, and any Additional Charges. In this example, the move is limited to a ten-mile radius, includes the use of padding and blankets, but has Additional Charges for stairs over two flights, appliance moves, or if items must be shuttled by smaller truck to the final destination (not uncommon for long distance moves).

All of the above items should be discussed with the moving company when you contact them for an initial quote or estimate for the cost of the move. No company worth hiring should be unable to answer any of these questions.

Another matter to discuss pertains to Insurance. Most movers provide a Base Amount of insurance, in this example, $10,000. You'll also want to inquire about the cost of Additional Insurance and whether insurance is based on Damage Value or Replacement Value.

Once you've covered all the basics, it's time to get an actual quote or Cost Estimate. In this example, the cost is $40 per hour per mover for two movers which equates to $80 per hour. Based on a three-room move, the company is estimating 3.5 hours which equals $280 ($80 x 3.5 = $280). Additional Charges include $25 for stairs and $25 for appliances as well as $5,000 in additional insurance at $10 per $1,000 or $50. So the total estimate equals $280 for labor and $100 in incremental expenses ($25 + $25 + $50 = $100) for a grand total of $380. Be sure to get this pre-move Cost Estimate in writing.

General Information:

Number of Rooms to Move	3
Pricing Methodology	Per hour
Number of Movers	2
Type of Payment Required	Cash or credit card
Limit on Distance of Move	10 miles
Use of Blankets and Padding	Yes

Additional Charges:

Stairs vs. Elevator	$25 if stairs over two flights
Heavy Items (i.e., appliances)	$25 for appliance move
Long Distance Move	$100 to transfer items to smaller truck

Insurance:

Base Amount	$10,000
Additional Insurance	$10 per thousand
Damage Value or Replacement Value	Replacement value

Cost Estimate:

Cost Per Hour		$40
Number of Movers	×	2
Total Cost Per Hour		$80
Estimated Hours	×	3.5
Base Cost		$280
Plus: Additional Charges (stairs)	+	$25
Plus: Additional Charges (appliance)	+	$25
Plus: Additional Insurance ($5,000)	+	$50
Estimated Total Cost		$380

CREATE YOUR OWN WORKSHEET

PROFESSIONAL MOVERS WORKSHEET

Filling out your Professional Movers Worksheet is rather straightforward and is usually something that can be done in one fell swoop. In fact, if you are considering hiring a professional mover, you'll want to have the blank worksheet in front of you as you talk with each moving company you could potentially hire.

Ask the mover to provide the information for each line item starting at the top of the page and working your way down. It couldn't be more simple and easy. Clarify how they expect payment: cash on the spot or credit card in advance. Cover all the General Information issues and be sure to get sufficient answers to any and all potential Additional Charges.

Turn the questions to Insurance regarding Base Amount, Additional Insurance, and Damage Value versus Replacement Value and you're practically home free.

Finally, close the conversation be asking for a pre-move quote or Cost Estimate in writing. Have them fax or email the quote before you ever agree to hire them. When calculating the quote, the company may ask you for a few pieces of information such as Number of Rooms to Move, Distance of Move, and special situations (stairs, appliances, long distances, etc.) all of which are covered here on the Professional Movers Worksheet.

Once you've received the quote, it's time to do your own calculation to ensure that the estimate you've received makes sense. Multiply the Cost Per Hour times the Number of Movers and you'll have the Total Cost Per Hour. Multiply this by the Estimated Hours the mover provided (based on the Number of Rooms you provided) and you'll have the Base Cost. Be sure to add to this any Additional Charges and the cost of Additional Insurance if this is something you choose to have. Sum up the numbers and you'll have the Estimated Total Cost which should be right on top of the estimate you just received from the moving company. If there is a discrepancy, call them back immediately and have them walk you through their rationale to explain to you how they are calculating things differently.

Once you are comfortable that each mover is calculating things exactly the way you are, it'll be very easy to compare the various quotes from among all the moving companies and choose the one that is right for you.

	Mover #1	Mover #2	Mover #3
General Information:			
Number of Rooms to Move			
Pricing Methodology			
Number of Movers			
Type of Payment Required			
Limit on Distance of Move			
Use of Blankets and Padding			
Additional Charges:			
Stairs vs. Elevator			
Heavy Items (i.e., appliances)			
Long Distance Move			
Insurance:			
Base Amount			
Additional Insurance			
Damage Value or Replacement Value			
Cost Estimate:			
Cost Per Hour			
Number of Movers	×	×	×
Total Cost Per Hour			
Estimated Hours	×	×	×
Base Cost			
Plus: Additional Charges	+	+	+
Plus: Additional Charges	+	+	+
Plus: Additional Insurance	+	+	+
Estimated Total Cost			

MONTHLY CAR BUDGET WORKSHEET

You've decided to buy or lease a car. The real question is not what kind of car do you want but rather, what can you realistically afford? This worksheet will help you answer that question so you'll know if you should be out shopping for a fancy sports car or if it makes better sense to get a compact car.

The examples starts with Monthly Gross Income of $2,000. Multiply this amount by 40% or 0.40 to arrive at the Amount Available for Rent, Car, and Debt of $800. The 40% figure is a standard guideline percentage that finance companies typically allow purchasers to spend on Rent, Car, and Debt combined.

Once you know you have $800 as the Amount Available for Rent, Car, and Debt, you need to subtract the other expenses to determine what is left for your Monthly Car Budget. Subtract your monthly Rent of $500 and the Monthly Debt Service of $100 and you are left with a Monthly Car Budget of $200. Now you know how much you can afford to spend each month when you are out shopping for a car.

Monthly Gross Income	$2,000
Recommended % to Spend on Rent, Car, and Debt	× 40% (or 0.40)
Amount Available for Rent, Car, and Debt	$800
Less: Rent	− $500
Less: Monthly Debt Service	− $100
Monthly Car Budget	$200

CREATE YOUR OWN WORKSHEET

MONTHLY CAR BUDGET WORKSHEET

You want a new car but you need to figure out how much car you can afford. Start with your Monthly Gross Income. As a reminder, if you only have an annual salary, divide this figure by 12 to arrive at your Monthly Gross Income. If you are paid by the hour and work 40 hours per week, multiply your hourly wage times 160 hours (40 hours per week × approximately 4 weeks per month) to determine your Monthly Gross Income.

Once you have your Monthly Gross Income, multiply this by the Recommended % to Be Spent On Rent, Car, and Debt of 40% or 0.40. The result goes on the line next to Amount Available for Rent, Car, and Debt.

Fill in the amount of your monthly rent on the Rent line. Do the same for the amount you typically spend each month on your credit cards and other debt and enter this amount on the Monthly Debt Service line. Subtract the Rent and Monthly Debt Service figures from the Amount Available for Rent, Car, and Debt and you will arrive at the amount of your Monthly Car Budget.

Monthly Gross Income

Recommended % to Spend on Rent, Car, and Debt   ×   40% (or 0.40)

Amount Available for Rent, Car, and Debt

Less: Rent   −

Less: Monthly Debt Service   −

Monthly Car Budget

CAR SELECTION TEMPLATE

After making the rounds to numerous dealers, you've decided that you want a sedan. Great! Now the question is, which one? The Car Selection Template is designed to highlight all the various car features and give you a chance to rate several of them in order to compare one sedan to another so you can make the most informed decision.

Start with the obvious, Year and Make/Model of the car, in this case, a 2003 Volkswagen Jetta. Two key numbers on the sticker of every new car on the lot are Price of $18,910 and Fuel Economy of 24/31 miles per gallon. You've quickly filled in the basics without even speaking to a salesman.

The next criteria are subjective and are based on your personal opinion. After all, you're the one buying the car, you should have an opinion about the car's Performance, Image, and your impression of the Dealership/Salesman based on your interaction when shopping and test-driving the car.

The remainder of the items on this template deal with the standard features and available options for a given model. If they are standard, such as Automatic Transmission, Power Locks, and Front Air Bags, they will be listed on the sticker on the window of the car. Optional items such as Power Windows, CD Player, and Sunroof, may be listed on the sticker as well. Regardless, the salesman should be able to answer all your questions about what features are available. Be sure to fill out every item on this template for each car you consider buying so you'll have a complete list to compare when you make your decision.

Year	2003
Make/Model	Volkswagen Jetta
Car Classification	Sedan
Price	$18,910
Fuel Economy (City/Highway)	24/31
Performance (1-10 scale)	7
Image (1-10 scale)	7
Dealership/Salesman (1-10 scale)	6
Transmission (Auto/Manual)	Automatic
Air Conditioning	Yes
Windows (Power/Manual)	Power
Seats (Power/Manual)	Manual
Locks (Power/Manual)	Power
Mirrors (Power/Manual)	Manual
Cruise Control	Yes
Stereo System	CD
Tires	All Weather Radial
Seating Capacity	4
Sunroof/Moonroof	None
Upholstery (Leather/Fabric)	Fabric
Steering Wheel (Adjustable)	Yes
Rust Proofing	None
Trim Package	Standard
Air Bags (Front, Dual, Side)	Front
Traction Control	Yes
Anti-Lock Brakes	Yes

CREATE YOUR OWN TEMPLATE

CAR SELECTION TEMPLATE

The Car Selection Template allows you to compare the features and specifications of up to three cars at the same time. It is extremely helpful to see a side-by-side comparison of a few different models when determining which car to buy. In order to make the most informed decision, fill out the template in as much detail as possible. If the information isn't listed on the sticker, ask the salesman.

The first five items, Year, Make/Model, Car Classification, Price, and Fuel Economy are straightforward. Pay attention to the next three: Performance, Image, and the Dealership/Salesman. These are subjective and require you to really think about your experience.

First is performance. You can really only determine the car's performance by test-driving it. How does it handle? Is it a smooth ride? What about acceleration? Basically you're trying to determine the overall "feel" of the car and your impression of it. Rate the Performance of the car on a 1–10 scale and write it down.

Image is another subjective test. Do you like the overall look of the car? Can you see yourself behind the wheel of that particular Make/Model for the next several years? What about the color? Make sure you're comfortable with the car. Rate this aspect on a 1–10 scale as well.

Next rate the Dealership/Salesman on the same 1–10 scale. Now what does this mean? How helpful has the salesman been? Is he receptive to your questions? Does he seem willing to help you figure things out or is he just pushing to make a sale? What's your overall impression of the "sales" experience so far? When making a purchase of this magnitude, be comfortable with the salesman and rate the dealer on a 1–10 scale which will be helpful come decision-making time. Remember, you still have to negotiate the price of the car.

The remainder of the items on this template deal with the standard features and available options for a given model. If they are standard, such as Automatic Transmission, Power Locks, and Front Air Bags, they will be listed on the sticker on the window of the car. Optional items such as Power Windows, CD Player, and Sunroof, may be listed on the sticker as well. Regardless, the salesman should be able to answer all your questions about what features are available. Be sure to fill out every item on this template for each car you consider buying so you'll have a complete list to compare when you make your decision.

	Car #1	Car #2	Car #3
Year			
Make/Model			
Car Classification			
Price			
Fuel Economy (City/Highway)			
Performance (1-10 scale)			
Image (1-10 scale)			
Dealership/Salesman (1-10 scale)			
Transmission (Auto/Manual)			
Air Conditioning			
Windows (Power/Manual)			
Seats (Power/Manual)			
Locks (Power/Manual)			
Mirrors (Power/Manual)			
Cruise Control			
Stereo System			
Tires			
Seating Capacity			
Sunroof/Moonroof			
Upholstery (Leather/Fabric)			
Steering Wheel (Adjustable)			
Rust Proofing			
Trim Package			
Air Bags (Front, Dual, Side)			
Traction Control			
Anti-Lock Brakes			

CAR LEASING TERMS

So you're thinking about leasing a car? Intimidated? Don't be. Car dealers use a lot of fancy terms and throw around a lot of numbers and it can all be quite confusing at first. The reality is that it's not nearly as complicated as it may appear to be.

The following is a list of the actual leasing terms used in the industry and by the dealers. Familiarize yourself with these terms and refer back to them as you go through the Car Leasing Worksheet. For a more detailed description of lease terms and aspects involved in the process, refer to Chapter 12: Leasing A Car in *Real Life 101: A Guide To Stuff That Actually Matters*.

Acquisition Fee – Up-front fee that covers a variety of administrative costs, such as obtaining a credit report and verifying insurance coverage.

Capitalized Cost Reduction – The sum of any down payment, net trade-in allowance, and rebate used to reduce the gross capitalized cost.

Depreciation – A vehicle's decline in value over the term of the lease. This is based on year, make, model, mileage, and overall wear.

Disposition Fee – A "restocking fee" the dealership charges to clean, detail, tune up, and return your car to inventory to sell as a used car when your lease is up.

Excess Mileage Charge – Fee for miles driven over the maximum annual limit specified in the lease agreement. The excess mileage charge is usually between $0.10 and $0.25 per mile.

Excess Wear and Tear Charge – Charge to cover wear and tear on a leased vehicle beyond what is considered "normal." The charge may cover both interior and exterior damage, such as upholstery stains, body dents and scrapes, and tire wear beyond the limits stated in the lease agreement.

Fees and Taxes – The total amount you will pay for taxes, licenses, registration, title, and official (governmental) fees over the term of your lease. Because fees and taxes may change during the term of your lease, they may be stated as estimates.

Gross Capitalized Cost – The agreed-upon price of the car before any down payment, rebate or discount. Think of it as the negotiated "sticker price" for the car.

Lease Term – The period of time for which a lease agreement is written, usually expressed in months.

Money Factor – The money factor is roughly equivalent to the annual interest rate divided by 24. For example, a money factor of 0.00333 equals an annual interest rate of approximately eight percent ($0.08 \div 24 = 0.00333$). Sometimes dealers don't mention the decimal places in a money factor, assuming that you will know that the decimal places are implied. For example, if the money factor is .00333, the dealer might simply say the money factor is "333."

Rent Charge – The financing component of the lease. It is the interest you are being charged to "rent" the car over the course of the lease.

Residual Value – The estimated value of the car at the end of the lease term. It is determined up front in part by using residual value guidebooks but is also negotiable.

CAR LEASING WORKSHEET

You've decided to lease a car. You've reviewed the Car Leasing Terms on pages 48–49 and feel comfortable with the lingo. Now it's time to calculate just what your Monthly Lease Payment will be. The example starts with Gross Cost (the price of the car) of $20,000. Subtract the Capitalized Cost Reduction (down payment) to get the Adjusted Capitalized Cost. In this case, since the Capitalized Cost Reduction is $0, the Adjusted Capitalized Cost is also $20,000. Subtract the Residual Value of $12,500 from this amount to get the Depreciation Value of $7,500. The Residual Value is the amount the car is estimated to be worth at the end of the lease term when you return the car. You have the option of buying the car at this price at that time. The Residual Value is given to you by the dealer but can be open for negotiation.

Back to the Depreciation Value of $7,500. Divide this amount by the Term of Lease, 36 months, and you have the Depreciation Component of $208. Follow the arrow down the page and enter the $208 Depreciation Component below.

Now calculate the interest you're being charged or Finance Component. Start with the $20,000 Adjusted Capitalized Cost (from above) and this time add the $12,500 Residual Value (also from above) to arrive at the Total Finance Value of $32,500. Here's where things get a little tricky. Dealers introduce a concept called the Money Factor. It is simply an annual interest rate divided by 24. An assumed interest rate of 10% (or 0.10) divided by 24 yields a Money Factor of 0.004167. Multiplying the Total Finance Value of $32,500 by the Money Factor of 0.004167 gives you a Finance Component value of $135. This is how much interest you're being charged each month to lease the vehicle. Follow the arrow and enter the $135 Finance Component below as well.

Now simply add the $208 Depreciation Component to the $135 Finance Component and you now know that this particular car will have a Monthly Lease Payment of $344.

Monthly Lease Payment:

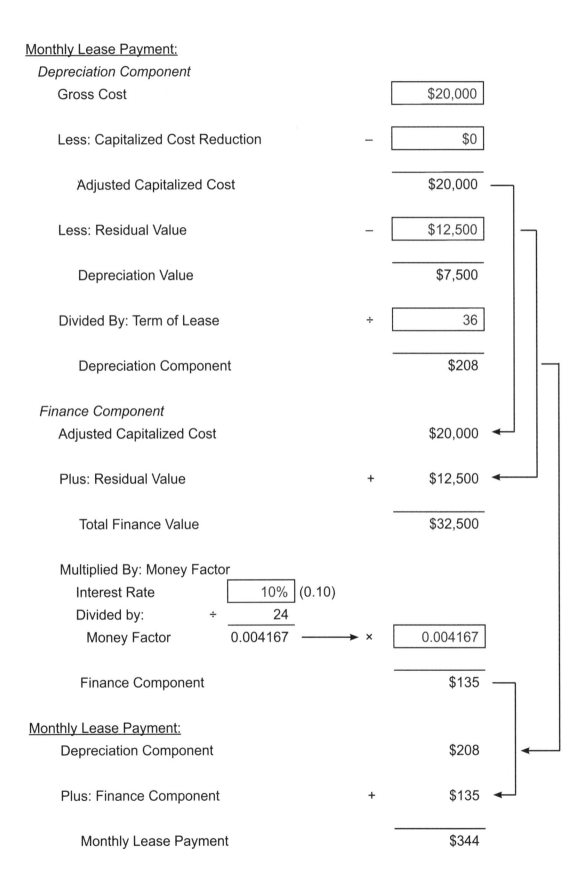

Depreciation Component

Gross Cost		$20,000
Less: Capitalized Cost Reduction	−	$0
Adjusted Capitalized Cost		$20,000
Less: Residual Value	−	$12,500
Depreciation Value		$7,500
Divided By: Term of Lease	÷	36
Depreciation Component		$208

Finance Component

Adjusted Capitalized Cost		$20,000
Plus: Residual Value	+	$12,500
Total Finance Value		$32,500

Multiplied By: Money Factor

Interest Rate	10%	(0.10)
Divided by:	÷	24
Money Factor	0.004167 →	×	0.004167
Finance Component		$135

Monthly Lease Payment:

Depreciation Component		$208
Plus: Finance Component	+	$135
Monthly Lease Payment		$344

CREATE YOUR OWN WORKSHEET

CAR LEASING WORKSHEET

What is the Monthly Lease Payment going to be on the new car you want? Start with the Depreciation Component. This is the monthly payment you would make if the dealer didn't charge you any interest. Subtract any Capitalized Cost Reduction from the Gross Cost to arrive at the Adjusted Capitalized Cost. Subtract the Residual Value and you have the Depreciation Value of the vehicle. Divide the Depreciation Value by the Term of Lease (always in number of months, i.e. 36, 48, 60, etc.) to get the Depreciation Component of the lease. Follow the arrow and enter this same figure again below.

Now for the Finance Component. Start with Adjusted Capital Cost (from above) and add the Residual Value (also from above) to get the Total Finance Value. Now for the Money Factor. If you're given the Money Factor, simply enter it on this line. Otherwise, if you're given an Interest Rate then do the mini-calculation. Enter the Interest Rate and then divide it by 24 to get the Money Factor. Once you have the Money Factor, multiply the Total Finance Value by the Money Factor to get the Finance Component. Follow the arrow and enter this same figure again below.

Now simply add the Depreciation Component to the Finance Component and you have the amount of the Monthly Lease Payment.

Monthly Lease Payment:

Depreciation Component

Gross Cost

Less: Capitalized Cost Reduction −

Adjusted Capitalized Cost

Less: Residual Value −

Depreciation Value

Divided By: Term of Lease ÷

Depreciation Component

Finance Component

Adjusted Capitalized Cost

Plus: Residual Value +

Total Finance Value

Multiplied By: Money Factor

Interest Rate

Divided By: ÷ 24

Money Factor → ×

Finance Component

Monthly Lease Payment:

Depreciation Component

Plus: Finance Component +

Monthly Lease Payment

COST PER THOUSAND DOLLARS BORROWED CHART

You'll need this chart as part of the calculation to determine your Monthly Payment when buying a car. Two components of the car loan are needed to use the chart—the Interest Rate and the Term of Loan.

In the example provided in the Car Buying Worksheet on page 57, the Interest Rate is 10% and the Term of Loan is 36 months or three years. The corresponding figure that is based on 10% and three years is $32.27. To arrive at this figure, find the row for a 10% Interest Rate. It's the bottom one. Now find the column for the loan period of three years or 36 months. It's the second column. The intersecting box of the bottom row and second column represents a 3-year loan at a 10% interest rate and indicates $32.27 as the Cost Per Thousand Dollars Borrowed.

Try another example, say an Interest Rate of 6% on a 4-year loan. In this case the Cost Per Thousand Dollars Borrowed is $23.49. In other words, you'll pay $23.49 each month for every $1,000 you borrow.

What do you do if the Term of Loan or Interest Rate you've negotiated with the car dealership doesn't appear on the chart? Here is an example of how to use the chart to solve other situations that are not explicitly laid out on the chart. Say you have a loan with a 4-year term at 8.5% interest. Well, 8.5% is between 8.0% and 9.0%. Look up each of these to assist you in the calculation. Four years at 8.0% is $24.41 and four years at 9.0% is $24.89. Now add $24.41 plus $24.89 to equal $49.30. Divide this amount by two and you get $49.30 / 2 = $24.65. This amount is the Cost Per Thousand Dollars Borrowed for a four-year loan at an 8.5% Interest Rate. As a check, remind yourself that $24.65 is between $24.41 (at 8.0%) and $24.89 (at 9.0%).

Flip things around and assume that the Interest Rate is fine but the Term of Loan doesn't match up with the chart. Assume a 4.0% loan for 4.5 years. Again, keep the 4.0% constant and calculate both a 4.0-year loan and a 5.0-year loan. 4.0% at 4.0 years yields a $22.58 cost per month per thousand. 4.0% at 5.0 years yields a $18.42 cost per month per thousand. A quick average of $22.58 plus $18.42 = $41.00 and then dividing by two ($41.00 / 2 = $20.50) results in a $20.50 per month per thousand dollars for a 4.0%, four-and-a-half-year loan.

Whatever Term of Loan and Interest Rate you are given, this chart will allow you to determine the Cost Per Thousand Dollars Borrowed and will help you to calculate your Monthly Car Payment.

Term of Loan

	2 Years (24 Months)	3 Years (36 Months)	4 Years (48 Months)	5 Years (60 Months)
0.0%	$41.67	$27.78	$20.83	$16.67
1.0%	$42.10	$28.21	$21.26	$17.09
2.0%	$42.54	$28.64	$21.70	$17.53
3.0%	$42.98	$29.08	$22.13	$17.97
4.0%	$43.43	$29.52	$22.58	$18.42
5.0%	$43.87	$29.97	$23.03	$18.87
6.0%	$44.32	$30.42	$23.49	$19.33
7.0%	$44.77	$30.88	$23.95	$19.80
8.0%	$45.23	$31.34	$24.41	$20.28
9.0%	$45.68	$31.80	$24.89	$20.76
10.0%	$46.15	$32.27	$25.36	$21.25

Interest Rate

CAR BUYING WORKSHEET

So you've decided to buy a car. You already know the price—it says so right there on the sticker. Of course, you're going to do your best to negotiate with the salesman to try and pay less than sticker, but either way, when the dust settles, you know exactly how much you're going to pay for the car. The point of this worksheet is to calculate how much you'll be paying each and every month.

Start with Gross Cost of $20,000 (this amount may actually be lower than the sticker price if you were successful in negotiating a lower price) and subtract the $2,000 Down Payment to get the Adjusted Cost of $18,000. This is the Amount Financed. Divide this $18,000 by 1,000 to determine the Number of Thousands Financed. This figure, 18, will come into play in a moment so follow the arrow and enter the number 18 below.

The next two boxes contain information based on what your dealer or finance company has told you about the terms of the loan you expect to receive. Enter the Interest Rate of 10% and the Term of Loan of 36 months (always in months) in the two boxes. You will need both of these components in order to look up the Cost Per Thousand Dollars Borrowed. Refer to the chart on Page 55 to determine this figure based on the Interest Rate and Term of Loan in the example.

Now multiply the 18 (Number of Thousands Borrowed) by $32.27 (Cost Per Thousand Dollars Borrowed) and you have the Monthly Car Payment of $581.

Monthly Car Payment:

Gross Cost		$20,000
Less: Down Payment	−	$2,000
Adjusted Cost		$18,000
Amount Financed		$18,000
Divided By: 1,000	÷	1,000
Number of Thousands Financed		18
Interest Rate		10%
Term of Loan (in months)		36
Cost Per Thousand Dollars Borrowed* *(see page 55)		$32.27
Number of Thousands Financed		18
Multiplied By: Cost Per Thousand Dollars	×	$32.27
Monthly Car Payment		$581

CREATE YOUR OWN WORKSHEET

CAR BUYING WORKSHEET

Time to calculate how much your new car is going to cost you each month. Start with Gross Cost of the car and subtract any Down Payment you will make to get the Adjusted Cost. Enter this number as the Amount Financed and divide it by 1,000 to get the Number of Thousands Financed. Follow the arrow and enter this figure below.

Now enter both the Interest Rate and the Term of Loan (in months) in the next two boxes. Using these two figures, turn to the chart on Page 55 to determine the Cost Per Thousand Dollars Borrowed. Enter the correct amount here as well as two lines below.

Finally, take the Number of Thousands Financed and multiply it by the Cost Per Thousand Dollars Borrowed to compute the amount of your Monthly Car Payment.

Monthly Car Payment:

Gross Cost

Less: Down Payment   −

Adjusted Cost

Amount Financed

Divided By: 1,000   ÷   1,000

Number of Thousands Financed

Interest Rate   %

Term of Loan (in months)

Cost Per Thousand Dollars Borrowed*
*(see page 55)

Number of Thousands Financed

Multiplied By: Cost Per Thousand Dollars   ×

Monthly Car Payment

CAR LEASING/BUYING CLOSING MONEY WORKSHEET

Whether you decide to lease or buy a car, you'll be required to pay a significant amount of money at closing just to drive the car off the lot. Unfortunately, the amount is not simply the down payment as there are several other fees and expenses you are required to pay.

Start with the Capitalized Cost Reduction/Down Payment since they are both the same thing with different names depending on whether you lease or buy. In this example, assume you lease and the Capitalized Cost Reduction is $0. Next on the list is First Monthly Payment of $250. You would then also add any Refundable Security Deposit that may be required (for a leased vehicle) but in this case this amount at $0 as well.

The next three items are essentially unavoidable. Add Initial Title Fees of $100, Initial Registration Fees of $500, and Sales/Use Tax of $1,000 to the list of expenses and fees due at closing. There is not much you can do to avoid these fees since they are government-imposed and controlled by the individual state in which you live. Occasionally, dealerships run promotions whereby they agree to waive these fees. In reality, they are not really waiving the fees since the government must be paid no matter what, the dealer is dropping the fees from your cost of the vehicle and paying the taxes himself in order to entice you to buy or lease the car.

Finally, add any Acquisition Fee (which occasionally appear in leases) which is $0 in this example and any Other Fees that may apply. The Other Fees line item is also $0 because it is rare that there are additional taxes or fees besides what are already included in this worksheet. Adding up all these items gives you a total of $1,850 which is the Total Due at Start of Lease/Buy Agreement.

Capitalized Cost Reduction/Down Payment	$0
First Monthly Payment	$250
Refundable Security Deposit (Lease)	$0
Initial Title Fees	$100
Initial Registration Fees	$500
Sales/Use Tax	$1,000
Acquisition Fee (Lease)	$0
Other Fees +	$0
Total Due at Start of Lease/Buy Agreement	$1,850

CREATE YOUR OWN WORKSHEET

CAR LEASING/BUYING CLOSING MONEY WORKSHEET

Whether you lease or buy, you'll have certain fees and expenses which must be paid prior to driving the car off the lot. Fill in this worksheet beforehand and you'll know exactly how much you owe the dealer on Day 1.

First is the Capitalized Cost Reduction (if you're leasing) or Down Payment (if you're buying). Next item is First Monthly Payment. You've already calculated this amount on a previous worksheet, so jot down this amount here. The Refundable Security Deposit applies only to leases but it is a negotiable item so even if you do lease, there is a good chance that this item can be waived. If not, enter this amount here.

The next three items are required by law and set by the state. During certain sales promotions, dealerships can sometimes "waive" these amounts. They're not really waiving them so much as they are releasing you from paying the taxes and they will pay the amounts due themselves as a sales incentive to get you to buy or lease the car. For the most part though, these are your responsibility. Enter the amounts for Initial Title Fees, Initial Registration Fees, and Sales/Uses Tax on the next three lines. The dealership should be able to provide these amounts.

The last two items are less common. Acquisition Fees usually apply only to leases and very often can be waived. If the dealer does suggest an Acquisition Fee, do your best to negotiate the removal of this fee. Minimize this fee with an ultimate goal of $0. Finally, list any Other Fees that may be a part of the total due at signing.

Once you have listed all the possible fees and taxes, add them up and you'll know exactly how much money you need the day of signing in order to drive off the lot in your new car.

Capitalized Cost Reduction/Down Payment

First Monthly Payment

Refundable Security Deposit (Lease)

Initial Title Fees

Initial Registration Fees

Sales/Use Tax

Acquisition Fee (Lease)

Other Fees   +

Total Due at Start of Lease/Buy Agreement

HEALTHCARE INFORMATION TEMPLATE

Health insurance can be confusing and difficult to understand. There are so many aspects regarding the types of plans, costs, coverage, premiums, networks, etc. So when selecting healthcare or even once you already have it, it's a good idea to list all of the features and nuances of your health insurance so you can be sure you understand everything involved.

Start by listing the Type of Insurance, in this example, a Preferred Provider Organization or PPO. Note that you'll pay a flat rate of $65 per month and there is no Deductible.

Other features to record include the frequency of Preventative Care and Checkups which in this case is twice a year. Also note the cost for Office Visits and Prescription Drugs. This particular PPO has $10 co-pays for Office Visits and charges $15 for Prescription Drugs.

For major medical expenses such as Inpatient Hospital Services, related Physician Visits, Medical Tests and X-rays, and Outpatient Surgery, be sure to record if these services must be performed in-network and what amount of the expense you would be required to cover if such care were received out-of-network.

Finally, indicate which types of treatment and medical attention will be covered by your insurance. In this example, items such as Maternity and Well-baby Care are covered while Physical Therapy and Dental Care are not covered.

	Covered	Notes
Type of Insurance		PPO Plan
Cost/Premium		$65 per month
Deductible		N/A

Covered Medical Expenses:

	Covered	Notes
Preventive Care and Checkups	√	Twice a year
Office Visits	√	$10 co-pay
Prescription Drugs	√	$15 per prescription
Physician Visits (i.e., in hospital)	√	In network (100% out of network)
Inpatient Hospital Services	√	In network (100% out of network)
Outpatient Surgery	√	In network (100% out of network)
Medical Tests and X-rays	√	In network (100% out of network)
Physical Therapy		No
Chiropractic Treatment		No
Drug and Alcohol Abuse Treatment	√	Yes
Rehabilitation Facility Care		No
Home Healthcare Visits		No
Skilled Nursing Care		No
Speech Therapy		No
Maternity Care	√	Yes
Well-baby Care	√	Yes
Dental Care		No
Mental Healthcare	√	Yes

CREATE YOUR OWN TEMPLATE

HEALTHCARE INFORMATION TEMPLATE

Understanding health insurance is no easy task. One way to get a handle on things is by listing all the specifics of a plan on this Healthcare Information Template. By so doing, you'll know all of the key features of your insurance program and what is and what is not covered. However, this template should not be a substitute for reviewing all the materials and information provided by your health insurance company.

Start by listing the Type of Insurance such as an HMO, PPO, or POS. Next, jot down the Cost or Premiums you'll pay each month for the insurance. Another financial component of your healthcare is the amount of the Deductible you'll be required to pay in the event you seek medical care under a Fee-For-Service plan. Record this number as well.

There are two other figures of note. Depending on the Type of Insurance you've selected, you may be required to make co-payments for each Office Visit as well as for any Prescription Drugs you receive. Be sure to write down these amounts on the proper line.

With the finances out of the way, turn your focus to all the various types of medical care and procedures you might need should you require medical attention. Go through the entire list of Covered Medical Expenses and check off those services that are covered by your healthcare plan.

In the Notes section, add pertinent information such as the frequency of Preventative Care and Checkups. For major medical expenses such as Inpatient Hospital Services, related Physician Visits, Medical Tests and X-rays, and Outpatient Surgery, be sure to record if these services must be performed in-network and what amount of the expense you would be required to cover if such care were received out-of-network.

By listing the major components and information regarding your health insurance on one template, you'll know exactly how you are covered and can rest easy should you ever need medical attention.

	Covered	Notes
Type of Insurance		_____
Cost/Premium		_____
Deductible		_____

Covered Medical Expenses:

	Covered	Notes
Preventive Care and Checkups	☐	_____
Office Visits	☐	_____
Prescription Drugs	☐	_____
Physician Visits (i.e., in hospital)	☐	_____
Inpatient Hospital Services	☐	_____
Outpatient Surgery	☐	_____
Medical Tests and X-rays	☐	_____
Physical Therapy	☐	_____
Chiropractic Treatment	☐	_____
Drug and Alcohol Abuse Treatment	☐	_____
Rehabilitation Facility Care	☐	_____
Home Healthcare Visits	☐	_____
Skilled Nursing Care	☐	_____
Speech Therapy	☐	_____
Maternity Care	☐	_____
Well-baby Care	☐	_____
Dental Care	☐	_____
Mental Healthcare	☐	_____

CHECKING ACCOUNT COMPARISON TEMPLATE

When selecting a bank and a checking account, you need to understand the differences between the various choices. This template helps you do that.

Each feature is important. Start with Minimum Balance Requirement, in this case $100. Next understand that you are only allowed 10 checks per month. You want to ensure that your account has a Check Card or Debit Card and has Online Banking Capabilities as well. Also confirm whether the account offers Paycheck Direct Deposit.

Finally, inquire as to the Monthly Fee, in this example $5.50, and the Non-network ATM Fee of $1.50 per transaction. And realize that for all of this, you're only allowed to interact with a human teller twice a month.

The point is to list all of the features of a given checking account next to other accounts in order to make the best decision as to where to transact your banking.

	Details
Minimum Balance Requirement	$100
Number of Checks Allowed Per Month	10
Check Card/Debit Card	Yes
Online Banking Capabilities	Yes
Paycheck Direct Deposit Available	Yes
Monthly Fee	$5.50
Non-network ATM Fee (per transaction)	$1.50
Human Teller Interactions Per Month	2

CREATE YOUR OWN TEMPLATE

CHECKING ACCOUNT COMPARISON TEMPLATE

With your checking account, you are looking for functionality and performance, but it is important to compare all aspects of an account in order to select the one that is right for you and meets your banking needs.

Start with the Minimum Balance Requirement. How much of your money do you want to be required to be in your checking account at any given time? Most people answer as little as possible. This could be a key factor as you evaluate various checking account options.

Next is Number of Checks Allowed Per Month. There is no right or wrong answer here. Some people do all their banking online and do not write a single paper check each month. For them, this category is irrelevant. For others, it is critical. Jot down the permissible amount to allow you to compare accounts.

The next three criteria of a checking account are "extras" that appeal to some customers and not others. A simple Yes/No on each line will suffice. Does the account provide a Check Card/Debit Card? Is the account set up for Online Banking? Is Paycheck Direct Deposit Available? Perhaps these items are vitally important to you. Perhaps you couldn't care less. Either way, find out the information and record it here. You want to know as much as possible before making a decision. Besides, it's possible that what is not important to you today could matter tomorrow.

Finally, note the Monthly Fee charged just for having the account open and the Non-Network ATM Fee. Here is where numbers can really matter.

One last figure to jot down is the number of Human Teller Interactions Per Month. This might not seem like a big deal in this age of ATMs and computers, but every now and then it is nice to have the safety of knowing that you can speak to a person face to face about whatever issues may arise and not have to pay for it.

Use this template to compare up to three checking accounts at three different banks before deciding which institution and which account is right for you.

	Bank #1	Bank #2	Bank #3
Minimum Balance Requirement	_____	_____	_____
Number of Checks Allowed Per Month	_____	_____	_____
Check Card/Debit Card	_____	_____	_____
Online Banking Capabilities	_____	_____	_____
Paycheck Direct Deposit Available	_____	_____	_____
Monthly Fee	_____	_____	_____
Non-network ATM Fee (per transaction)	_____	_____	_____
Human Teller Interactions Per Month	_____	_____	_____

CREDIT CARD ACCOUNT COMPARISON TEMPLATE

There are so many providers of credit cards and so many different types of cards with so many varied features that determining which is right for you can be overwhelming. With all the credit card advertisements and offers it can be difficult to cut through all the clutter and find out which card is preferable to another. This template will help you do that.

Start with Type of Card, in this case it is a Visa card. Next is Annual Fee of $50. You pay this fee each and every year regardless of how much or how little you use the card.

Many credit card providers have begun offering their cards with a promotional low interest rate as a way of enticing new subscribers. You need to understand the two key features of this promotion. The Introductory Interest Rate of 2.9% and the Length of Introductory Period of six months.

Once this promotion is over, the Long Term Interest Rate of 14.9% kicks in. This is the true interest rate you'll be paying for the rest of the time you have the card. Remember that balances you build up during the Introductory Period at the Introductory Interest Rate of 2.9% will switch to the higher Long Term Interest Rate of 14.9% once the Introductory Period is over.

Another feature credit card issuers offer to attract new customers is the ability to Transfer Balances onto New Card. Say you had an existing credit card with a $500 balance outstanding and were paying 16.9% interest. This new credit card would allow you to transfer that $500 balance from your old card to the new card and you would now be paying only 14.9% (and perhaps even the low 2.9% Introductory Interest Rate depending on the credit card issuer's offer). Note that there is a Balance Transfer Fee of 3.0% of the amount transferred or $15 ($500 x 3.0% or 0.03 = $15).

Finally, one of the biggest promotional features credit card issuers use to attract and keep customers are the Perks they offer with a particular card. This card is affiliated with American Airlines and provides American Airlines Frequent Flier Miles just for using the card. Typically, you receive one mile for each $1 you spend on the card. Credit card issuers have aligned themselves with nearly every airline, hotel chain, major retailer, automotive manufacturer, etc. Whatever your interest, there is likely a credit card with a Perk to meet your needs.

	Details
Type of Card	Visa
Annual Fee	$50
Introductory Interest Rate	2.9%
Length of Introductory Period	6 months
Long Term Interest Rate (following intro period)	14.9%
Transfer Balances onto New Card	Yes
Balance Transfer Fee	3.0% of amount transferred
Perks (e.g., mileage program)	American Airlines Miles

CREATE YOUR OWN TEMPLATE

CREDIT CARD ACCOUNT COMPARISON TEMPLATE

With so many credit cards available and so many offers and solicitations coming at you from all directions, it's best to lay out all your options before deciding which card to choose. This template allows you to compare the features of three different cards at once.

Start with Type of Card. There is Visa, MasterCard, American Express, Discover, and several others. The only real difference with respect to preferring one over another has to do with where you'll be using the card. Not every retailer or merchant accepts every type of card. Keep this in mind when making your selection.

Next is Annual Fee which can range from $0 to $100 or more; there is no typical fee or standard amount. Often, cards with Perks charge higher fees while cards without Perks have little or no Annual Fee. Jot down the amount of the fee on the line even if it is $0.

Credit card issuers are determined to attract new customers. One of the most popular promotions is to offer an Introductory Interest Rate. It is a very low interest rate, much lower than the standard Long Term Interest Rate. When evaluating new card offers, note the Length of Introductory Period. After this period, the interest rate reverts (jumps up) to the Long Term Interest Rate. One card may have a low 2.9% Introductory Interest Rate for six months and then have a permanent 16.9% interest rate. Another may offer a 4.9% Introductory Interest Rate for nine months and then have a permanent 14.9% interest rate. Which one is right for you depends on your situation.

Another feature is the ability to Transfer Balances onto New Card. This feature is handy if you have an existing credit card with an outstanding balance at a higher interest rate. The new card will transfer this outstanding balance from your old card to the new one so you could pay less in interest and save money. Record whether the card has this feature and if so, also note the Balance Transfer Fee. This is usually a percentage of the amount transferred such as 3.0% but sometimes is a flat fee of say $25 regardless of the amount.

Finally, you need to understand the Perks offered by the card. For some people this is the most critical aspect of a credit card while for others it doesn't matter at all. Traditional Perks include airline frequent flier miles and hotel points but Perks now include items from retailers, automobile manufactures, and service providers. The point is that different Perks exist for practically everyone. Note all the Perks on this template to assist you in your comparison of credit cards.

	Credit Card #1	Credit Card #2	Credit Card #3
Type of Card	_____	_____	_____
Annual Fee	_____	_____	_____
Introductory Interest Rate	_____	_____	_____
Length of Introductory Period	_____	_____	_____
Long Term Interest Rate	_____	_____	_____
Transfer Balances onto New Card	_____	_____	_____
Balance Transfer Fee	_____	_____	_____
Perks (e.g., mileage program)	_____	_____	_____

MONTHLY BILLS WORKSHEET

The process of paying bills can be a time-consuming hassle. With so many different bills due at various times of the month, it can be difficult to keep on top of things and ensure that you pay each bill on time. The only way to do this is to have a system. This worksheet will help you get organized.

Start with all of the bills facing you each month. Write down when each bill is due. For example, Rent is usually due on the 1st of the month. Your Car Payment and Car Insurance might be due on the 30th of every month. Other bills may come at intervals throughout the month such as Phone on the 15th, Electricity on the 28th, and Credit Card #2 on the 19th. With all of these different due dates, you have to list them on your Monthly Bills Worksheet in order to keep track of everything.

Once you have the worksheet set up, you need to record the amount you pay for each bill as you write the check or make the payment. Some of the items such as Car Payment will be the same $225.45 each and every month. Other bills, like the Phone, will $24.75 one month and a different amount the next month. By filling in the amount you pay each month, not only will you ensure that you pay the bill on time, but at the end of the year, you'll have a complete record of what you've paid for each and every bill.

	Due Date	January
Rent	1st	$500.00
Car Payment	30th	$225.45
Car Insurance	30th	$70.75
Health Insurance	30th	$121.51
Phone	15th	$24.75
Electricity	28th	$17.95
Cable	15th	$34.50
Internet	15th	$20.95
Water	30th	$12.95
Gas	30th	$14.10
Cell Phone	28th	$35.00
Credit Card #1	28th	$50.00
Credit Card #2	19th	$75.00
Total Monthly Bills		$1,202.91

CREATE YOUR OWN WORKSHEET

MONTHLY BILLS WORKSHEET

Keeping track of all your monthly bills makes sense for several reasons. You want to ensure that you actually pay each and every bill so you're not evicted from your apartment or your car isn't repossessed. You also want to make sure that you pay your bills on time to avoid late fees and additional interest charges. Finally, at the end of the year, having a complete list of all your expenses can be useful when reviewing where you've spent your money and when budgeting for the coming year.

Start by listing all of the bills you have each month. First are big items such as Rent, Car Payment, Car Insurance, and Health Insurance. Next are all of your utilities such as Phone, Electricity, Cable, Internet, Water, Gas, and Cell Phone. Finally, don't forget about any Credit Cards or Other expenses.

Now that you've listed all of your monthly obligations, you need to jot down when they are actually due. First of the month, middle of the month, last of month, or any date in between—whatever the due date, make a note of it on this schedule.

Once you have the worksheet set up with all of your bills and the dates on which they are due, you're all set. Now the most important thing to do is to actually fill in the worksheet whenever you pay each bill.

By filling in the amount you pay for each expense, you'll be certain to pay each bill on time and avoid any late fees or additional interest charges. Be diligent about completing the worksheet and you'll be on top of your financial responsibilities each month and at the end of the year, you'll have a complete record of your expenses for the entire year.

	Due	Jan	Feb	Mar	Apr	May	Jun	Jul	Aug	Sept	Oct	Nov	Dec
Rent													
Car Payment													
Car Insurance													
Health Insurance													
Phone													
Electricity													
Cable													
Internet													
Water													
Gas													
Cell Phone													
Credit Card #1													
Credit Card #2													
Other													
Total Monthly Bills													

USEFUL CHECKLISTS

MOVING CHECKLIST

	Completed
Organize everything before starting to pack	☐
Make a list of furniture and large items	☐
Do a little "spring cleaning" (i.e., get rid of some stuff)	☐
Clarify all costs and details of truck rental	☐
Buy all moving supplies in advance of the move (i.e., boxes and blankets)	☐
Purchase specialty boxes (e.g., wardrobe box)	☐
Arrange for the rental of a dolly or hand truck	☐
Fill out change of address forms with the post office and utility companies	☐
Schedule utility hook-up appointments	☐
Pack by room	☐
Label each box on the front, left-hand corner	☐
Record each item on the master packing list	☐
Spread heavier items (e.g., books) throughout several boxes	☐
Box up all loose items (e.g., telephone, remote controls, sports equipment)	☐
Load large items into the truck first (i.e., mattress, couch, TV)	☐
Secure all items in the truck	☐

KITCHEN ITEM CHECKLIST

	Have	Need
Kitchen Items:		
Dishes – Set of 4	☐	☐
Glasses – Set of 4	☐	☐
Silverware – Set of 4	☐	☐
Pots – 3-Quart Saucepan with Lid	☐	☐
Pans – 7" or 10" Frying Pan	☐	☐
Pitcher – 2-Quart	☐	☐
Sharp Cutting Knife	☐	☐
Cutting Board	☐	☐
Colander	☐	☐
Cookie/Baking Sheet	☐	☐
Wooden Spoon	☐	☐
Plastic Spatula	☐	☐
Rubber Spatula	☐	☐
Wine Corkscrew	☐	☐
Spices/Condiments:		
Salt	☐	☐
Pepper	☐	☐
Oregano	☐	☐
All-purpose Seasoning	☐	☐
Sugar	☐	☐
Vegetable Oil	☐	☐
Ketchup	☐	☐
Mustard	☐	☐
Mayonnaise	☐	☐
Salsa	☐	☐
Salad Dressing	☐	☐
Pantry Items:		
Sponge	☐	☐
Mop	☐	☐
Broom	☐	☐
Dish Towels	☐	☐
Vacuum Cleaner	☐	☐
Toilet Brush	☐	☐
All-purpose Cleaner	☐	☐
Glass Cleaner	☐	☐
Tub and Tile Cleaner	☐	☐
Toilet Bowl Cleaner	☐	☐
Disinfectant	☐	☐
Dishwasher Soap	☐	☐
Dish Soap	☐	☐
Laundry Detergent	☐	☐

TEST-DRIVE CHECKLIST

	Examined	Rating or Notes
Overall Feel of Car	☐	_____
Front Seat Legroom	☐	_____
Front Seat Headroom	☐	_____
Back Seat Legroom	☐	_____
Seat Adjustment	☐	_____
Mirror Vision	☐	_____
Non-Mirror Vision (i.e., side and rear views)	☐	_____
Dashboard Controls	☐	_____
Lights/Brights	☐	_____
Turn Signals	☐	_____
Windshield Wipers	☐	_____
Brake Lights	☐	_____
Slow Speed Handling	☐	_____
Braking and Turning	☐	_____
Parallel Parking	☐	_____
Smoothness of Ride	☐	_____
Acceleration	☐	_____
Passing Capability	☐	_____

USED CAR INSPECTION CHECKLIST

	Examined	Rating or Notes

Exterior:
- Overall Appearance
- Body
- Trim
- Paint Job
- Rust
- Salt Corrosion
- Windshield
- Doors, Trunk, Hood
- Tires
- Lights, Brights, Brake Lights
- Turn Signals
- Wipers

Interior:
- General Condition
- Upholstery
- Seat Belts
- Seats
- Windows
- Locks
- Horn
- Dashboard Controls
- Clock
- Sound System
- Heater/Air Conditioner

Under The Hood:
- Belts and Hoses
- Fluids
- Oil
- Battery
- Spark Plugs
- Air Filter

Mechanical Inspection

CAR INSURANCE SELECTION CHECKLIST

Details
_____

Make/Model
_____

Year
_____

Parking (garage, street, covered, etc.)
_____

Mileage To Work
_____

Mileage Per Year
_____

Driver Details (age, sex, driving record)
_____

Amounts
_____

Bodily Injury Per Person
_____

Bodily Injury Total
_____

Property Damage
_____

Comprehensive Coverage
_____

Personal Injury Protection (No Fault)
_____

Uninsured Motorist Coverage
_____

Medical Insurance Coverage
_____

Rental Car Coverage
_____

Annual Cost of Insurance
_____

Deductible
_____

CAR MAINTENANCE SCHEDULE CHECKLIST

	Frequency	Mileage	Examined	Notes
Tire Pressure	Monthly	–		
Lights	Monthly	–		
Lube/Oil Change and Filter	3 Months	3,000-7,500		
Belts and Hoses	3 Months	3,000-7,500		
Brakes	6 Months	6,000		
Air Filter	6 Months	7,500-15,000		
Rotate Tires	6 Months	6,000		
Wheel Balance	6 Months	6,000		
Wheel Alignment	1 Year	12,000		

GLOSSARY

Acquisition Fee – Up-front fee that covers a variety of administrative costs, such as obtaining a credit report and verifying insurance coverage.

Capitalized Cost Reduction – The sum of any down payment, net trade-in allowance, and rebate used to reduce the gross capitalized cost.

Collision Insurance – Covers damage to your own vehicle in an accident. Often optional according to state laws, it is likely to be required under a lease or when financing a purchase.

Comprehensive Insurance – Covers damage to your vehicle other than collision such as fire, flood, theft, and vandalism. Like collision coverage, this is often optional according to state laws, but is likely to be required under a lease or when financing a purchase.

Co-payment – A small fee you pay for each doctor's visit or prescription under a managed care insurance program.

Depreciation – A vehicle's decline in value over the term of the lease. This is based on year, make, model, mileage, and overall wear.

Disposition Fee – A "restocking" fee the dealership charges to clean, detail, tune up, and return your car to inventory to sell as a used car when your lease is up.

Excess Mileage Charge – Fee for miles driven over the maximum annual limit specified in the lease agreement. The excess mileage charge is usually between $0.10 and $0.25 per mile.

Excess Wear and Tear Charge – Charge to cover wear and tear on a leased vehicle beyond what is considered "normal." The charge may cover both interior and exterior damage such as upholstery stains, body dents or scrapes, and tire wear beyond the limits stated in the lease agreement.

Family Practice Physician – Treats all family members (adults and children) and may include maternity care.

Fee-For-Service – Insurance under which you pay a small premium and then only for what services you use. You pay every dollar up to the deductible amount and then your insurance "kicks in." Typically, once you have reached the deductible, the insurance company pays 80% of medical expenses and you pay the remaining 20%.

Fees and Taxes – The total amount you will pay for taxes, licenses, registration, title, and official (governmental) fees over the term of your lease. Because fees and taxes may change during the term of your lease, they may be stated as estimates.

Flexible Spending Account – A special account where you can contribute money before it is taxed. These pretax dollars can then be used for medical expenses such as contacts and prescriptions depending upon your specific healthcare plan.

General Liability Insurance – Covers injuries and/or death that may result from an accident. Each state has different minimum requirements.

General Practice Physician – Provides care not limited to a specialty.

Gross Capitalized Cost – The agreed-upon price of the car before any down payment, rebate, or discount. Think of it as the negotiated "sticker price" for the car.

Health Insurance Premium – The amount you pay for health insurance. It can be paid monthly, quarterly or annually.

Health Maintenance Organization (HMO) – A managed care program that utilizes a network including a primary care physician. To be covered by your HMO, all medical care must be performed by doctors and hospitals affiliated with the network and your primary care physician must refer you to any specialists. When service is provided "in network" you pay only the small co-payment. If you go "out of network" you may be responsible for 100% of the medical expenses.

Heath Insurance Deductible – The minimum amount you pay each year before the insurance company begins paying its portion.

Internist – Focuses on nonsurgical diseases in adults.

Lease Term – The period of time for which a lease agreement is written, usually in months.

Managed Care – Insurance under which you pay a higher premium but there is no deductible. Instead, you pay a co-payment amount each time you utilize medical services. The three types of managed care are HMOs, PPOs, and POS plans.

Money Factor – The money factor is roughly equivalent to the annual interest rate divided by 24. For example, a money factor of 0.00333 equals an annual interest rate of approximately eight percent (0.08 ÷ 24 = 0.00333). Sometimes dealers don't mention the decimal places in a money factor assuming that you will know that the decimal places are implied. For example, if the money factor is .00333, the dealer might simply say the money factor is "333."

Network – Under a managed care plan, a group of affiliated doctors and hospitals from which you choose your primary care physician and where you receive your medical care.

OB/GYN – Specializes in obstetrics and gynecology for women.

Ophthalmologist – Concentrates on eye disorders and treatment of eye disease.

Optometrist – Evaluates visual capacity and fits appropriate lenses.

Pediatrician – Oversees care for infants, children, and adolescents.

Personal Injury Protection (No Fault) Insurance – Covers the cost of injuries to you or your passengers resulting from an accident regardless of who was at fault. Many states require this type of coverage.

Point of Service Plan (POS) – A managed care program that is a combination of both the HMO and the PPO. Like an HMO, you are required to select a primary care physician. Like a PPO, if you go "out of network" you are responsible for 20% of the costs. Similar to both plans, if you stay "in network" you pay only the co-payment amount.

Preferred Provider Organization (PPO) – A managed care program that utilizes a network but does not typically require you to choose a primary care physician. Like an HMO, when you stay "in network" you are only responsible for the co-payment. The difference is if you go "out of network" the program acts like a fee-for-service plan. That is, the insurance company would pay 80% and you are responsible for the remaining 20%.

Premium/Deductible Relationship – Lower the healthcare deductible, the higher the premiums.

Primary Care Physician – The doctor you see for regular check-ups and who coordinates and directs all of your medical needs including referrals to specialists.

Rent Charge – The financing component of the lease. It is the interest you are being charged to "rent" the car over the course of the lease.

Residual Value – The estimated value of the car at the end of the lease term. It is determined up front in part by using residual value guidebooks but is also negotiable.

Uninsured Motorist Insurance – Covers you if you are in an accident with a party who carries insufficient or no liability insurance. Some states require this coverage.

W–2 (Form W–2) – Recap of annual gross income and all taxes paid.

For More Information or
To Order Additional Copies Please Visit:

www.galtindustries.com